QUIET TIMES

QUIET TIMES

You are the Light

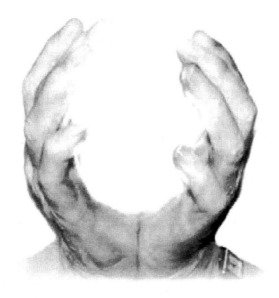

Rev. M.E. Logan

To order additional copies of this book, contact:
Xlibris Corporation
1-888-795-4274
www.Xlibris.com
Orders@Xlibris.com
58448

Contents

Introduction

For years in the '60s I had a time of meditation that I referred to as my *quiet time*. In the early '70s when I began to study for the ministry my *quiet time* changed and I began to write poetry almost every morning. When I became pastor of a small church in 1978 my life and my quiet time changed again. The *quiet time* now was for prayer and guidance which in many times helped with individuals as well as church services.

There were times when a church member was struggling with a problem, a poem would begin with some thoughts for encouragement and guidance. Some helped in times of bereavement. More times than not, it was about God's love without exception for each of his creations.

Finally, through the help and encouragement of my sons and a close friend the words are in print so others might share the harvest of my quiet time.

"The Beginning Of My Day"

I am so very happy.
My heart is full of praise
For the love God shows me
In, oh so many ways.

He gives me peace and freedom
And more strength as I pray
In the glow of the morning
As I begin my day.

Then there is the tender look
Upon my loved one's face.
My grandson's angel smile
Can set your heart apace.

The gentle touch of a friend
As he passes by my chair.
Kind words from a stranger
Echoes a note of care.

My sweet daughters-in-law
That really are my friends.
The trust that is given
The counsel that I lend.

The list is never ending
So I'm sure you'll see
I believe every day is
Thanksgiving Day for me.

"The Country Church"

I saw a country church
Nestled in some cedar trees,
I went inside to rest
And set my mind at ease.

As I knelt down in prayer
A child tiptoed gently in.
Quietly he watched me;
His hands cupping his little chin.

When I sat upon the bench
He came close to me.
"I never saw you here before,
Whoever might you be?"

I am a weary nomad
And far away from home.
I've wandered here and there
Still further I must roam.

"Sir, whatever you are seeking,
May I help you in your search?
Perhaps we can find it
By praying in this church."

How could you, a mere child,
Help me in my quest?
If I should accept help
It must be the very best."

"I will pray to the Father
And he will give you aid.
Sir, He'll forgive your sins
And make you unafraid."

Who gave you this wisdom
And understanding, mild?
What makes you think you know
The Father will help me, child?

"I do not have a doubt
That God will make you whole.
For my name is Jesus,
And I know within my soul."

"Gods Symphony"

The country seemed so peaceful
As I paused awhile to dream
Of how God paints the countryside
With his bright color scheme.

Suddenly, this quiet spot
Seemed to explode with sound.
And it grew more beautiful;
There was music all around.

The gentle breeze blew softly,
Rustling the falling leaves.
A meadow lark called to her mate
Far above the trees.

A squirrel chattered at a crow
Who was resting near.
The voice of a whippoorwill
Reached my listening ear.

The thundering waterfall,
It's beauty undenied,
Became a stream bubbling
Down the mountainside.

The cooing of the gray dove
Joined the joyous sounds;
To sing along in harmony
of how God's love abounds.

I thought how like the "Silence"
This scene proved to be.
When you're still and concentrate
You hear a symphony.

"The Christmas Gift"

As the Christmas season
Comes around again this year;
Feel the Master's presence.
Know that He is near.

He is there beside you
As you decorate the tree,
When you light the candles
And say a prayer for me.

His love shines forth through you
As the presents you prepare
For your friends and loved ones
Each chosen with such care.

Then on Christmas morning
We gather 'round the tree.
Filled with anticipation,
Wondering what the gifts might be

The children stand there waiting
For their gifts with glee.
Some are wrapped with ribbons;
Others hang upon the tree.

But the most precious gifts of all,
That no one else can see,
Are the gifts of the Spirit
That God has for you and me.

"The Golden Light"

The golden light of Jesus
Is coming now your way.
He'll guide you as you go,
In all you do and say.

He'll walk with you in shadows,
In sunshine and in rain.
He'll take away your cares
And also ease your pain.

Place your faith in Jesus
For your daily bread,
And in your life of spirit,
By His ways be led.

Jesus bids you, "Come,
Spend some time with me.
From all care and pain
My love will set you free."

So, please, don't tarry longer.
Hear the Master's urgent call.
He will bless your life
When you surrender all.

"Picking Up The Pieces"

I must pick up the pieces to this life of mine.
Put the ones that fit together in some kind of rhyme.
Some of the worn out ones I will have to let go;
They do not fit the pattern of the way that I must go.

The pathway has been hidden for so very long,
But now shows so clearly just where I do belong.
It stretches out before me as far as I can see.
It has no obstructions, this path through eternity.

I must hurry onward, not linger along the way.
There is so much to do and so very much to say.
As I teach God's children and help them all I can;
Showing how much He loves them, each and every man.

This work has been layed out for me for a long, long time.
Waiting for my eyes to open and begin this task of mine.
Anxious now to be about the learning of the way;
So that I might teach God's will forever and a day.

Even now that I understand there is no end to time,
It does not alter the urgency in the spiritual climb.
The sooner I begin, the more people I can reach
With these simple lessons the Lord gives me to teach.

"Easter Morning"

As I awake this Easter morning
There is no one else around.
I rise to meet the Christ
In this new life I have found.

As He rose from the tomb
To show there is no death;
He shows me every day
How God is closer than my breath.

Jesus came to free us
From the bonds we had attained.
Beliefs in limitation
Should never be entertained.

With God there is no limit
To the things that we might do,
When we follow as he leads us
In everything we do.

As we wait for his instructions
For the path we are to take;
There comes a peace within,
Knowing he makes no mistakes.

Listen to the gentle urgings,
Follow every lead.
The Christ is ever longing
To fill your every need.

"Beyond The Golden Gate"

A friend of mine just passed
Through that golden gate beyond,
Leaving me with memories
Of which I am very fond.

I never will forget him;
I would be a fool to try.
For we will meet again,
So I'll not even cry.

There will be a note of sadness
When I remember him
And wish that we could talk
About the times that might have been.

But, I know that when my time comes
My friend will be waiting there.
Then we will talk of yesterday
And of how much we care.

We will not need to hurry
Or fear the time will end,
For beyond the golden gate
There is always time for friends.

"The Veil between Us"

I would like to be your Valentine
As I was once, long ago.
Be able to hold your hand
And let my love for you show.

But, there is a veil between us,
You cannot see my face.
Still this great love I feel
No one can ever replace.

Your face is there before me.
As I watch you go along,
Someone else now lights your eyes
And gives your heart a song.

I pray he will be gentle
And someday, really care;
Then your lives will be complete
With a love beyond compare.

Valentines are meant to share
With the ones we truly love;
To tell them how much we care,
Even though we've gone above.

"The Garden"

There blooms a love garden
Within my very soul
Since God has blessed me
With His touch of purest gold.

As my thoughts go out to others,
A bouquet of love imparts
A healing meant for all
Who know the Lord within their hearts.

God cultivates this garden
And showers it with care.
So when the flowers bloom
They go out on wings of prayer.

These flowers of love will heal
A troubled state of mind,
Or mend a broken body,
Or a lost soul find.

This garden in my heart
Was meant for me to share,
Because you see, my dear,
God's love is everywhere.

"In The Fathers Way"

Take some time to worship;
Take some time to pray.
In the quiet stillness,
Hear what I have to say.

You mustn't hurry, scurry;
Just set your mind at peace,
The time is coming soon
When you will find release.

Don't fret and second guess me;
Just trust me all the way.
Then everything will work out
In the Father's way.

"Heaven's Door"

Jesus is the eternal pattern
Of the way God would have us live.
As to you He has freely given,
To others you must freely give.

As you begin to follow
This as your way of life,
Troubles will seem to drop away;
Love will ease all strife.

You will be feeling better
Than you ever have before.
Your whole life will be brighter
Once you open Heaven's door.

"Opening The Way"

The way has begun to open,
The kingdom of God is at hand,
Go forth and heal the sick
And teach throughout the land.

The work for you is endless;
Do only as I ask.
When there is one in need,
I'll give guidance for the task.

Never venture into something
Unless guidance is very plain.
We want to do the will of God,
Not look for material gain.

"The Early Morning"

Let me tell you now,
How I feel a thrill
When the morning comes
And the world is still.

Everyone is still asleep,
Not a soul is around.
Silently from my bed I creep
So as not to make a sound.

The house is very peaceful
When I turn to God in prayer;
Just a word with Him,
Telling Him how I care.

In silent meditation,
His turn it is to speak;
Assuring me of His love
With the guidance that I seek.

And in this quiet morning
The birds begin to sing.
Telling further of God's love
With a joyful note of spring.

The flowers seem to smile,
Nodding their heads to say
"God loves you so much,
He gives you blessings every day."

The sun comes slowly up
Sending it's warming rays
To fill my very soul
With the goodness of His ways.

Noises of the working world
Reach my listening ear;
Telling me that it is time
To take myself from here.

Now others I can help,
Perhaps even show the way,
That everything is better
When God begins your day.

"The Promise"

In the quiet of this morning, Lord,
As I begin this day,
Help me to still myself
As I commence to pray.

May I ever be humble
And loving as I speak;
Giving thanks and praise
For the guidance that I seek.

I bow in deep devotion
To the God that I adore,
Knowing that he understands
The aid I now implore.

The words that I would speak
Are between my God and me.
So, in silent communion,
we will together be.

Just a time of sweet communion
With no one else around;
A loving conversation held
Without uttering a sound.

I will gain more wisdom
From this precious meeting
Than all I would receive
Forever elsewhere seeking.

God has a great plan
For my serving life.
All I have to do is listen
And He'll set aside all strife.

The words he would have me hear
Are in the silence spoken;
Assuring me of His guidance,
Which never can be broken.

God will bless you in the morning,
He heals throughout the day;
He wants to make you fully whole
In every possible way.

"The Gentle Understanding"

Let me lead you onward
To the road that Jesus trod;
We will heal the sick
And teach the ways of God.

Let us be about our business
To do His work and will.
It is the path you've chosen
To the kingdom on the hill.

The raising of the consciousness
Is the beginning of the way.
This is accomplished slowly,
By going to God each day.

In the morning when we rise
We start our day with prayer;
Communion with our Lord
Will surely help us there.

Each time that we reach up
To meet our God in prayer,
It will be a little easier
To tell others how we care.

God eases all our tensions
And our feet He will guide;
To gently walk the path
Till we reach the other side.

He teaches us to love all people
With the love that is of God.
A gentle, understanding way,
Like Jesus, son of God.

"The Holy Breath"

I have heard the gentle knocking
Of the Holy Breath upon my door.
I bid her a heartier welcome
Than any guest before.

If only she would enter and
Whisper wisdom to my soul,
That would be the happiest time
That's ever been foretold.

I have heard the gentle knocking
Of the Holy Breath upon my door.
The Lord has sent her to me
As He promised long before.

In the quiet of this morning
She comes softly in to me;
To tell of the many things
That God would have me see.

I know that she will linger
To tell the mysteries of old,
And in her tender loving way,
The sweetest story ever told.

"The Greeting"

I believe that worshiping God
Cannot be overdone,
So I arise to greet Him
Before the morning sun.

He is here in times of joy,
Also, in times of doubt.
Just that still, small voice within;
Never a need to shout.

He will always hear me;
Forever He is near.
He abides within my soul,
Of this I have no fear.

No one can ever harm me
Through malice or with hate;
For He is here to shield me.
He is the Master of my fate.

"The Conversation"

Talk to the Father.
Tell Him how you care.
Know that He is with you;
He is always there.

Hard times are nearly over,
You will find release.
There truly is no comfort
Like the Father's peace.

He stands there beside you
And guides you every day.
Still yourself and listen
To all that He might say.

Take this time of worship
As your daily bread.
Know that from His wisdom
You are always fed.

Talk to the Father
Quietly in prayer.
And in your heart remember
He is always there.

"My Special Place"

I always take my quiet spot
With me where 'ere I go.
Whenever I feel troubled
I reach for it and know
The peace that I am needing
Is never far away.
I just find my quiet spot
And take some time to pray.

"Have Faith"

There are times when we are weary
And times when we are tired.
All about us seems so dreary
That we feel totally uninspired.

Do not let these times of doubt
Get underneath your skin.
Things will turn out right
When you seek the peace within.

For within us is the answer.
We seek in faith to find,
To whatever seems to trouble us
And wreck our mortal minds.

Take it to the Christ in prayer.
He's the Master of your life.
He will bless and hold you
To ease the care and strife.

Never worry about the things
That threaten your peace of mind.
They will soon pass away
And leave no scars behind.

Place your trust in your Father-God;
Your thoughts in His loving care.
Know that He solves all problems;
Have faith that He is there.

"Be Strong"

Blessings on you, my son,
Your time of heartache is nearly done.
Keep the faith is all I ask;
I will help you with your task.

When you come on bended knee
I will answer your fervent plea.
The peace of God for you is there,
When you ask in earnest prayer.

I will help you all I can
To find the good in every man.
In the morning when you pray,
Listen to all that I might say.

Guidance for your life ahead
Helps you know there's naught to dread.
So take each day with peace and calm,
And faith in God is your healing balm.

"The Wondering Soul"

I bless you, child of God,
As I pray for you today,
With the health God meant for you
Before you went astray.

You started thinking idle thoughts
Of ill health and disease,
And now you reap the harvest
Of these carefully nourished seeds.

Let go of all limited thoughts;
Change your state of mind.
You have the power to heal yourself;
It lies dormant in your mind.

God gave you life that you might live
In abundance full and free.
Won't you restore it now to the state
God meant for it to be?

Dwell on the thought—
God created me
In body, mind and soul.
So now he can heal me,
And make me truly whole.

As these word of truth
Penetrate your soul,
You will be restored;
You will be made whole.

"The Light"

The light that rises in the sky
And flows down over me,
Is there for all God's children
When they begin to see.

As they open up their hearts
To do God's work and will;
Their lives begin to prosper
As each need he does fulfill.

The giving of one's self
Is all that He requires.
Then the Holy Spirit comes,
And their work inspires.

The Holy Spirit teaches them
All they need to know
To walk the streets of Heaven
And set their heart aglow.

So we will keep on praying
For the light that shines
To fill man's understanding
With God's love divine.

"Seek The Kingdom"

If you would seek His kingdom,
Don't journey far and wide.
God is waiting in the Silence
For you to turn inside.

His kingdom is close at hand;
It is never far away.
Thought it seems sometimes to be
As our consciousness does stray.

The gateway to the kingdom
Is swinging open wide.
The time has finally come
To hurry on inside.

No need to wait any longer
Outside the temple gate;
He is ready for you.
Please don't hesitate.

As soon as you enter the temple
All else will drop away.
Peace will fill your soul
And joy will fill your day.

"Glowing Wonders"

The sun is up and glowing;
It stirs my very soul
With the wonders of God's knowing
How faith will make me whole.

As the sun spreads it's light
All about the earth;
So God spreads His love
With a boundless rebirth.

"The Assurance"

You ask for faith and well you might;
Faith will help with any plight.
It is the assurance of God's love
And of all things that are above.

The tiff and toil of this old earth
That would hinder your rebirth
Assurance that God does His vigil keep;
He is not dead, He does not sleep.

Our welfare is His prime concern
This we constantly affirm
Our faith will gain in strength and grow
So the world we can show

When in the Master you confide
And in His ways you do abide,
The way is easier every day
That faith is there for which you pray.

"A Way Of Life"

Being a messenger of God
Is not a cross to bear,
For it is a pleasure
To tell people how He cares.

This is a way of life
To be carried on joyfully;
Teaching the ways to the kingdom
To those who will receive.

Jesus said "Take up my cross
And then do follow me,
You shall know the truth
And the truth shall set you free."

Come unto me all ye that labor
And I will give you rest.
I came to show the kingdom
To those who are hard pressed.

And so we will move onward
To free the souls oppressed;
Then by the Father's way
We truly will be blessed.

"Show Me The Way"

Jesus, please guide my steps aright
That I might not stumble in the night,
But with unbroken stride
Go forth in eternal pride
That you are the light that guides.
As my every thought in you abides,
Guide my thoughts that I might stay
In close communion every day
With the things you would have me know
To help others, the pathway show.

Grant the insight and the strength
To do all that is required.
Father, I ask for all in need
To be truly God inspired.
Help me to teach all mankind
The better way of life;
How everything is easier
When they set aside all strife.

Through Your holy love,
Lead me to do Your will;
Blessing everyone in sight
With a "Peace, be still."

"Sincerity"

You are a child of God, not limited in any way.
So go forth and heal the hearts of men, perhaps do it when you pray.
Pray for peace on earth and good will to your fellow man;
And I assure you that every time you do, these things will return to you again.

God loves you so very much and He wants you to happy be.
You do it by looking to the heaven and you do it with sincerity.
When you speak of Merry Christmas, merry you must be;
And never leave the Christ out of Christmas for that's the heart of it, you see.

Realize that Jesus was an example to show us a better way,
To talk about the Father being one with us and to still ourselves and pray.
So go aside from the noise and the clutter of the earth;
Still yourself and ask the Holy Spirit to help you with rebirth.

God Bless You.

"I Am The Giver"

I am the giver and the gift;
The very essence of you, you see.
So come again to yourself
and manifest more of me.

I gave you a body to live in,
To do with as you will.
You've neglected it and that
Was part of your mission to fill.

If you care not for the body
Then you're not using my gift supreme;
The gift of mind that is myself
That would fill your every dream.

You've let yourself run tired,
And always at a hectic pace,
To make up for the time you've wasted
As you sat looking out in space.

Come again to yourself
And you will happy be
When you realize our oneness;
Our oneness with eternity.

Come again to yourself and
Spend some time with me.
I will guide you on your way;
I will lead you tenderly.

You will find successes every day you live
When you wait for the internal guidance;
Then you will know for sure
That the Father truly does forgive.

Release Of Strife

Almighty Heavenly Father,
Praises I sing to your name;
And my memory strays to a time gone by
When I heard the words to this refrain.

I heard the voices of my loved ones
Blend and rise on high,
Singing praises to your glory
as they felt Your presence nigh.

I heard my brothers harmonize
On these words that I hold so dear,
But they walked a different path;
They no longer felt You near.

I followed along in Your footsteps
For a period of my life,
Then You took me by the hand
And said "Let's leave behind the strife."

We stepped back on that path again,
The one that leads to Thee,
And happiness reigns in this heart of mine;
I feel Your goodness rush through me.

I see the ways of error
Of those that I held so dear;
I beheld the trouble in your eyes
And in Your voice, the note of fear.

I behold the words of Tennyson
And the crossing of the bar,
And I thought if only they had heard Thee
Perhaps they would not have strayed so far,

But we release them to their paths
And tell them there's naught to fear,
As we walk on to living
And hope that they will hear.

They must forgive all things
Of the earthly plane
If they are to gain a moments rest,
Assurance that heaven they will gain.

Honesty

Father, teach them how wrong it is to lie
And say that they have,
When they have not; and they have not,
When they have plenty standing by.

Forgive them Father, for this error.
Help them to behold the right,
Say only words of truth
And state them with all their might.

That they may walk straight and tall
Unburdened from all care
And realize they have plenty;
Plenty and more to share.

For You are the tremendous giver,
The giver of all things,
And when we trust in You and You alone
What a plenty the world doth bring.

Father, it is needed
Every day in prayer,
A blessed assurance;
Let us feel Your presence there.

And have the Holy Spirit teach us
A better way for each one.
For when they cross into that next dimension,
They'll know of victories won.

Then not have to come back into a life
That is just like this one now;
Because they changed their way of thinking
And made a holy vow

To be true to themselves and others
While in this earthly life.
But it all began when they decided
To set aside the strife.

"Come Up A Little Higher"

The picture of Jesus is before you,
How bright and colorful He appears.
Right now He's looking into your heart
And what do you think He hears?

Think not that you can mask
The thoughts you carry day by day,
For He visits you in your home
And He hears the words you say.

He says "I love you dearly,
But I'm asking you right now
To come up a little higher;
I ask for a holy vow.

I ask that you change your way of thinking
And the things you say and do;
To lead a pure and holy life
Treating others, not as they treat you,

But the way you would be treated
By anyone on this earth.
Put aside negativity
And strive for all you're worth.

Ask that divine love fill every part
Of your mind, your body and your soul,
And the healing that you say you longed for
Is yours, it will make you whole.

Divine love is not just for the other fellow,
For order or justice that is true,
But what you mete out
Is what returns to you."

God lives inside of each of us,
You and the Christ and God are one.
Realize your Christhood
As a victory won in Christ.

Healing Meditation

Now, I picture some place in the center of my mind
That, in my spirit, each one of you I stand just behind.
With a holy, heavenly essence I anoint you in this place;
Perhaps you can feel a trickle down your hair or on your face.
I see as that essence touches you that relaxing does now appear.
I see the tension dissolving from the top of your head to your ear.
I see that relaxation travel down to that tight held neck;
Then I see it spread down your shoulders and down your back.
I see that relaxation move down through your biceps and forearms,
Down through your hands and fingers, releasing that tightness that harms.
Then in my mind's eye, back to your neck attention now is gained;
We see it relax, not once, but again and again.
This relaxation travels down through your chest and your waist;
Of course it follows that it goes down your back again, making a little base.
Down through your abdomen and your hips this relaxation now does go,
And then down through your legs; out of them this relaxation now does flow.
I see the tension moving out of your ankle, too;
I see that relaxation following and pushing that tension from you.
Now it goes to those feet and toes releasing all negativity,
And as it does this realize, from all tension you now are free.
It's dispersed into the universe, never to come back again.
You are now ready for your healing and the healing of your fellow man.
I would have you behold someone, someone that you hold quite dear;
I would have you see a light above them and whisper to them "there's naught
    to fear".
For you see, there is fear held tight within them, they can't seem to let it go.
They are fearful of their future, for the Christ they do not know.
Then I would have you behold another, perhaps someone that's just a name;
I'd have you surround them with a light and maybe make it a holy game.
Now see it around another and ask for blessings through and through,
For everyone that comes to mind right now or for some of the things you want
    to do.

Ask that God's richest blessings bless your heart and mind,
And ask to be forgiven for thoughts of a negative kind.
Realize that what you ask of others will, in turn, be asked of you.
So be careful what you seek after, be careful that the motive is true.
For I assure you that all thoughts that go out from us
Return in kind, and sometimes we make quite a fuss
Because they are not to our liking and comfort. But yet we do not see
That we've put this in motion by the thoughts inside of you and me.
So concentrate on that radiant light, the light of eternal God.
He will bless your heart and mine, and then there's a spiritual nod;
A "go ahead" with those plans you have, and the good is there for you.
If it's really meant to be yours nothing can keep it from you.
You are God's beloved child and to Him He holds you dear;
And He says "Just trust and wait, for truly, I love you, my dear."

Healing Thanksgiving

Heavenly Father, we give thanks for that life that flows through us.
Teach us to bless it many times a day so that it will flow to the fullest,
to the truest, to the purest.

And we give thanks for that light that is given us that we may know
The path to follow and the place to go.
And bless the love that we may feel free to give more and receive more.

Amen.

Crystal Butterfly

I've come to say hello to you and I want you to just relax;
Behold in your mind's eye a crystal from which the light refracts.
You see those pretty colors as they penetrate the heart of you,
And realize as that crystal spins that yours is a different hue.
Each and every color abides everywhere in space,
But is the color really there until it shows upon your face?

I come as a crystal butterfly and as I wing my way to you,
I'd like to be a guide of yours; to show you what to do
To find your way to the inner chamber, the one that's deep inside,
Not on a lofty hill nor on a mountainside.
Because it's a chamber within you it surely can't take much space,
But I tell you this and I tell you now, there is glory in this place.

This place is inside your temple, you can see your crystal there.
The light within you illumines it, it grows brighter when you're in prayer.
The colors are dancing all about you, on the outside and within,
And the more you behold the colors, the sooner the process begins.
When you concentrate on the lights that were put there by our God,
You will see a change within you when your eyes are lifted from the sod.

Lift your eyes to the heavens when you venture deep within;
When the colors appear to you there will be silence, not a din.
But in the silence, that silence of the soul,
A voice, a thought will penetrate; sometimes a bell will toll.
Or then again, a different vibration, not a color or a sound,
Sometimes just a thought does there abound.

The earth winds are natural healers and they make that harmony within.
Now the troubled self can stay in a place where no sound has ever been.
Contemplate your thinking; ask for it to be made crystal clear,
And an inner voice will respond "As you wish it, so shall it be, my dear."
I bless you in this quiet time, I bless your body mind and soul.
Give thanks to the Creator, that He has made you whole.

Come Again To The Kingdom

Come again to the Kingdom and linger for awhile.
When you leave, I guarantee, that you will wear a smile,
When you think of the Presence that manifested then;
And it's there every time you enter, again and again.

The Christ is always waiting for some time you have to spare
So He can have your ear to tell you that He cares.
Come inside to the Kingdom and spend some time with Me,
I love you so, my dear, and I will through eternity.

Eternity is not in the future, but right now, in this place.
You've been in it for so long, it exists without a trace.
Here and there, now and then, an elusive thing, I'd say,
But it is so very real, every single day.

You live in the eternal now and how you spend your time
Is molding all your future days, and whether or not they rhyme.
Come again to the Kingdom and join in thought with Me.
I will see you healed, this is a guarantee.

The Father's love and energy are waiting for you there;
When you call them forth, there's plenty for you to share.
Come with a wheelbarrow, basket or truck;
The healing you desire will raise you from the muck.

The mire of error thinking, that has dragged you down so low,
Will leave in an instant when you let it go.
I see that healing power twinkling here and there;
Waiting to come forth with your earnest prayer.

Come again to the Kingdom and I will let you see
All the things you've hoped for, and all the things you'll be.
Have faith in a mighty future, have faith in God and Me;
Have faith in yourself, my dear, for we are one, you see.

I love you all so very much, a love that can't be told;
But by a thought, a word, a touch—My presence makes you whole.
Come again to the Kingdom, spend some time with Me,
And from every ache and care My love will set you free.

In The Silence Of This Moment

In the silence of this moment that we set aside to pray
Let us begin by asking forgiveness of the things we've had to say,
Of the times that we have trespassed where we had no right to go,
Of the seeds that we had planted that we had no right to sow
In the quiet of this moment cast away each fear
And know that, to God the Father, you are always dear.
Take the time to consider those for whom you pray;
Be sure that you are kind and that you are loving in the things you have to say.
Pray for them to be made whole, not just mended now in part;
Make your prayers the feeling kind that come from the very heart.
Loose yourself from anger and free yourself from fear;
Trust only in the Father and know that He is near.
Free yourself from the bondage in which you live.
Instead of looking to get, look to see what you can give.
For its only in the giving that you in turn can receive;
It's only in the faith, that which you believe,
That in turn your life is guided, and then you are made whole
When you trust God the Father with your very soul.
When you worry about your fellow man, and what he takes away,
You receive less and less with each passing day.
Bless them with their taking and they will reap in kind,
But they'll not reap the harvest that one day you will find.
Deep within your soul, it's what you ought to ask,
And then for strength, to carry on your task.
Then our Heavenly Father will give these gifts to you,
And the sunshine of His blessing will shine on everything you do.
Look for the good in the now, put aside the pain of yesterday;
Look for a bright tomorrow and you'll find a brightened day.
Do not review the yesterdays, for it benefits you not
In the glories of tomorrow and can you ask for ought.
The healing of the Father will penetrate your soul,
Free you of fear and burdens and make you truly whole.

"My Love Is Here To Stay"

The Christ is always with you,
He does not walk away.
So trust Him when He tells you
"My love is here to stay."

Linger with Him in the morning,
Thank Him for your daily bread;
Know that He will heal you
As by His way you're led.

He guides you as you journey,
He watches as you sleep,
He comforts you in your sorrow;
Your loved ones He does keep.

Your painful times are over,
Your doubts are at an end;
Realize His goodness and
Count Him as your friend.

"The Teaching Of The Way"

Come inside and just relax,
Spend some time with me.
I will teach you all you need,
I will answer your every plea.

If you will listen closely
To all I have to say,
I will lead you onward
To the teaching of the way.

In the silence of the kingdom,
The inner reaches of the soul,
My words will lead you onward;
My words will make you whole.

"The Secret Path"

The Master walked that secret path
That led through the Massalian Grove.
He needed peace and quiet,
As for strength He strove.

Communion with the Father,
Seeking guidance for the task
That He was about to face,
Was not too much to ask.

God gave Him courage to go on
With His head held high,
And the assurance He needed
That He could not die.

Today the Master walks
That secret path with me;
Giving me strength and courage
To face each difficulty.

He assures me of His presence;
In a tender voice He speaks,
"Come, I will teach you the way
To the kingdom that you seek."

"Remember that you told me
Your life was mine to use;
Follow each instruction,
Don't tarry or refuse."

"I have chosen you to walk
This secret path with me,
Knowing you will not fail,
It is the path of victory."

So as we walk together
To teach and heal the blind,
We will demonstrate God's love
for all of mankind.

"Enter In"

Enter His gates with thanksgiving,
Enter His courts with praise.
Enter His loving kingdom,
Enter His heavenly ways.

Enter His daily blessings,
Enter His light divine.
Enter His holy temple,
Enter His peace sublime.

"The Masters Lullaby"

Last night as I was praying,
The Master came to me;
Quietly took my hand
And my troubles seemed to flee.

"Don't pray so hard and long,
Have faith and trust in me.
From all of your burdens
My love will set you free."

"Remember Me as your friend
Through trials, heartache and sorrow,
And I will always be there
to gladden your tomorrow."

"Together we can meet
Anything that might arise,
As long as the light of God
is shining in your eyes."

"Be still now and listen
To that still small voice within,
Guiding your every footstep;
each victory to win."

"Sleep now, my child,
Let my love in you abide.
Next time that you are troubled,
Know that I am by your side."

"The Tender Heart"

Tender hearts are made to be handled
With gentle, loving care.
They need to know, without a doubt,
Someone is always there.

"Tomorrow"

There is such a special place
That takes up neither time nor space,
It harbors not sadness or sorrow;
Only peace and happiness reign in Tomorrow.

The streets are not lined with gold,
Nor are there fortunes unforetold;
Treasures that you cannot borrow
are being stored for all in Tomorrow.

Perhaps if we would change today,
And strive to live the Master's way,
Trying only seeds of love to sow;
planting for our harvest in Tomorrow.

We would find the living today
Would be easier in every way,
Not thinking how hard a row to hoe,
but humbly trusting in tomorrow.

If you should think you're going to die,
And wonder whether a home on high
Or if some other place you'll go,
Be assured there is a Tomorrow.

Life goes on, it does not end,
On that you can rely, my friend.
This Jesus promised years ago,
There will always be a Tomorrow.

Trusting only in the Lord,
Knowing there's no need to hoard;
Merely trying each day to grow
in faith of a divine tomorrow.

Though some people call it heaven
And believe it a distant haven;
To those of us who know,
We call it simply tomorrow.

"My Words"

"Come unto me," said the Master,
"My truth will set you free,
If my words abide in you
And you abide in me."

What simple instruction,
But it is all that you will need,
To change your life completely
And make you free indeed.

You will know divine peace
in the kingdom of the soul.
When you seek and find it,
Your faith will make you whole.

The Master's Hand

Since the Master blessed my life
With the teaching of the way,
Miracles seem to happen
Each and every day.

It doesn't take great insight
To see the working of His plan;
How my life has prospered
By the Master's hand.

When, at last, I heard Him knock
And decided to let Him in,
He healed my very soul
And gave me peace within.

Then, in silent meditation,
He imparted wisdom from above;
That I might teach others
How to accept His love.

Next He fulfilled the needs,
From His ever abundant supply,
To ease my constant labor
For things that I must buy.

So when you hear the Master knock
I hope you will understand,
How your life can prosper
With the touch of the Master's hand.

"Wisdom In Footsteps"

His wisdom guides our footsteps in peace and serenity
As we teach His children the ways of eternity.
Of how life goes on forever and doesn't stop at all;
Even when we stumble, we don't have to fall.

The Master's hand is outstretched to help us o'er the way
Along the well trod path, made easier when we pray.
We must use Jesus as our pattern of the way that man should live;
Encouraging them to try harder, as they have much to give.

Teach that with forgiveness comes a peace of mind
That cannot be supplanted, it is the hallowed kind.
As the gift of His love divine we help them to understand,
Peace will begin to reign, blessing all throughout the land.

"Open To Receive"

This is the way of God;
All things He will provide
To those who do His bidding
And whose candle does not hide.

He will see that you receive
All things, both large and small,
To help bring His kingdom
And blessings to one and all.

"Quiet Time"

Won't you come and share
A quiet hour with me;
Ponder the ways of God
And how He would have us be.

We won't babble on,
But sit in silent prayer.
Feel the Master's presence
Telling us how He cares.

"When two or more touch
In holy thought with me,
The answer will surely come
To satisfy each plea."

"Tender Presence"

Master, take my hand,
Come and walk with me.
Let me feel your presence
Beside the tideless sea.

I need your tender presence
To calm my troubled soul,
Take away my depression,
Cleanse and make me whole.

Oh, my blessed Master, please
Spend this time with me.
Assure me of your presence,
For I need your company.

Help me to open doors
That have seemed locked tight,
As Your presence shows me
Halls of golden light.

I want to open every door,
Step through them one by one,
Knowing I am guided
By the presence of the Son.

"My Friend"

As I sat down to dream
A vision came to me,
About the life that I might have
And what I'd like to be.

Prayerfully, I asked,
"Lord, may I have your hand?
Show me the surest way
To this promised land."

There appeared before me,
In answer to my prayer,
An abundant life of Spirit
And joy beyond compare.

This has been my desire
For such a long, long time;
I scarce could catch my breath,
Seeing this scene sublime.

Then Jesus stood beside me
And I heard Him say,
"Come along, follow Me,
I am the chosen way."

He said, "I am the truth,
Abide awhile with me;
For when you know the truth,
That truth will set you free."

He said, "I am the life.
I come that men might live,
And truly live abundantly;
This gift is mine to give."

"I am here to guide you,
Whatever be your task.
The right way I will show you,
When you pause to ask."

The way unfolds before me
As I climb those golden stairs;
An abundant life of Spirit,
In answer to my prayers.

Stronger Grows The Way

The Master takes my hand
And walks along with me,
Through the quiet pastures
And along the stormy sea.

It matters not where I wander,
For He is always there,
To guide my every footstep
And tell me how He cares.

His light goes before me
So that I will know
Where the pathway bends
And which is the way to go.

As His light grows stronger,
The way I clearly see;
It stretches out ahead,
Throughout eternity.

So I will walk along
With the Master's hand on mine,
Knowing that the path ahead
Is made safe by my friend divine.

"A Walk With The Master"

As I walked with the Master
Beside the Sea of Galilee,
Something happened that transformed
The very heart of me.

He took away the pain
That had racked my weary soul,
And with one tender touch,
He cleansed and made me whole.

No longer will I doubt
That He really does love me;
From all kinds of grief
His truth has set me free.

My moral life was empty
And aimless, seemed to be,
But now life has a purpose
That even I can see.

To teach the ways of God
As they were taught to me,
While I walked with the Master
Beside the Sea of Galilee.

"Be Still And Know"

God's great love for His children
Is there for all to see.
So still yourself and just relax,
And come along with me.

We'll worship at the feet of God
And kneel down at the cross.
He will touch us and bless us;
All else we'll count as loss.

We will go on together
To teach the ways of God.
We will heal the sick;
By heaven we will be shod

So that we may tred lightly,
Not hurting others as we go.
The way to reach the kingdom
With kindness we will show.

Peace on earth, good will to man
Was the message Jesus brought.
Showing God's love for all
In everything He taught.

To follow in His footsteps
Is our one desire
To stay within His path
As we keep reaching higher.

He is the perfect pattern
For our way of life;
His light goes before us
To set aside all strife.

When listening in the silence,
Waiting for Him to speak,
We truly will receive
The guidance that we seek.

So let's begin to teach
The will that is of God;
Every need will be provided,
As ever onward we trod.

The road ahead is endless,
As is all of life itself,
But we shall never weary
For we have the Father's help.

"The Healer"

Whisper softly in my ear
All you would have me know;
Lessons in the way of truth,
So others I might show.

I will try to listen
Ever so carefully,
That I might not miss
One word that is meant for me.

Early in the morning
I'll meet you in the den.
Together we will gain the heights;
Never to sink down again.

I pray that I will be
A healer, tried and true.
There are so many people
Needing all that I might do.

I am a willing channel
For the power that is of God;
To heal the sick and wounded
And teach with a gentle prod.

As we continue to progress
And bless each one we see,
Our lives will be enriched
Beyond all capacity.

Thank you for all the help
That you daily give to me.
I couldn't get through one day
Without your guidance and totality.

"The Wayside"

As I sat along the wayside
A stranger paused to speak.
Such beautiful words He uttered,
About the freedom that men seek.

He told that if you're troubled
And peace seems far away,
Don't keep forever searching;
It's never found that way.

The secret to all life's mysteries,
Whether love, heartache or care,
Can be found deep inside
When you silently kneel in prayer.

So let's end this weary journey
And change life's very tide;
Listen to that wonderful stranger
As He speaks deep down inside.

Let's follow the pattern He showed us
And seek the life within;
Fill our lives with good
And leave no room for sin.

The doors to the kingdom will open
If you pause a while to pray;
Not just sporadically,
But faithfully each day.

"When I Rise"

I get a close, secure feeling in the morning, as I rise,
Just knowing that the Christ is right there by my side.
As I turn my thoughts to God, to thank Him for the night
And the multitude of things that will make this day so right;
The feeling of security grows as I place my trust in Him
For the loving guidance drawing me away from sin.

"The Every Need"

God gives everlasting peace to the followers of the way
When they look to Him for guidance in all they do and say.
Ever open channels to seek and do His will,
Knowing from His substance, their every need He'll fill.

They let their light so shine that everyone might see
The glory of the Father's work done in humanity.
They look to Him for life that will never cease
And He fills their heart with love that brings a Christmas peace.

You Are The Father's Child

When you are down and blue,
Feeling all out of sorts,
Remember, you are the Father's child.

When you have a beautiful day
That is too good to be true,
Remember, you are the Father's child.

When your body aches all over
And the pain is much to bear,
Remember, you are the Father's child.

When you have lost a dear one
And you are filled with sorrow,
Remember, you are the Father's child.

When you see the miracles of nature
And wonder how they came to be,
Remember, you are the Father's child.

When you feel a glowing love for the world and all mankind,
You won't have to stop and try to think;
You'll know, you are the Father's child.

"*Guidance*"

Listen to that still, small voice
As it whispers deep inside,
Giving you wise advice
That will turn the tide.

When you pay attention
With an ever listening ear,
With His love He will guide you;
Never have a fear.

Take the time to be aware
Of the guidance that He gives;
Then mistakes will not be made,
As in Him you live.

God's presence is ever with us,
No matter where we stray.
He is there to guide us
All along the way.

"Sweetness"

Morning is a fine time to sit quietly and pray,
Before the world awakes to confuse what you want to say.
Your mind is still at peace, refreshed from a night of rest;
Not bothered by the problems, you can see how you've been blessed.

Thank your God and praise Him for the quiet of the night,
And the tender way He leads you toward that ever shining light.
Cherish the sweetness of His presence; tell Him all you have to say;
No one ever had a better route in which to start their day.

"My Gift"

My gift is mine and yours is yours,
Tho' different they may be.
God picked that special one for you
And He chose this one for me.

So let us work together
To do His work and will;
Then everything will turn out right
And our glad hearts He will fill.

I'll pray for yours and you pray for mine,
That's the way that it should be;
For God wants us to love each one,
That's why He sent you to me.

The Master By My Side

Oh, to walk down that pathway
With Jesus by my side,
Fills me with such gladness;
My joy I cannot hide.

The doors to the kingdom
He throws open wide,
And secrets of the heavens
To me He does confide.

He tells me to forget all else
And in His love abide;
Assures me of His presence
Throughout the even' tide.

So I walk down that pathway
With a sense of pride;
Knowing no harm can befall me,
For the Master is by my side.

Lessons

I feel so deeply touched
As these words echo in my ears,
And on the Master's face
I can see the stain of tears.

I will follow His pattern
Now, as I kneel to pray,
Father-God, not my will,
But Thine, be done in me today.

My Journey

I have walked down so many roads
In this life of mine.
Sometimes I grow weary when I think
Of the mountains I must climb.

But since the Master touched me
And opened my blinded eyes,
The way is much smoother;
Filled with love and joy, not sighs.

His guidance levels mountains
And straightens the crooked ways;
Widens the narrow paths
And clears away the haze.

He shows me part of my future,
All that I need to know;
How I will teach His people,
The ways to His kingdom show.

He tells me to abide in Him
And do only as he asks;
The power and strength will be given
To complete God-given tasks.

So I'll not look for mountains,
Nor fear the stormy sea;
For I know the Master
Clears the way for me.

"Let Me Teach Them"

On the banks of the Jordan River.
The Master knelt to pray.
It seems that I can almost hear
The words He had to say.

"Father, please give Me the power
To fill their every need;
That they might understand
And in their lives succeed."

"Help Me to show them
How to live their lives day by day,
And make their load lighter
As they travel along the way."

"Oh, Father, help Me to teach them
Of the kingdom of the soul
And how to pray believing
So their faith can make them whole."

"I would like to demonstrate peace,
The kind that only You can give,
When man treats all with kindness
And learns how to forgive."

"Let Me explain the natural law
Of the harvest of the soul;
Then man can be more careful
About the seeds he will unfold."

For He knew about the heartache
In the path that laid ahead;
How Judas would betray Him
And the blood that He must shed.

Still, He knelt there praying;
He kept His eyes above
And put His trust in God,
This messenger of love.

"Father, thank you for everything—
The joy, the trials, the strife;
Because they help me to prove
That there is eternal life."

Fill yourself with thoughts of God,
Forget about the worldly things.
The time will be more usefully spent
Finding the key that God's love brings.

"Steadfast"

The Master bids me, "Come,
Spend some time with Me.
I'll listen to your cares,
And from them set you free."

"Don't look to these mortals
For the love you need;
Divine love will suffice
And make you free, indeed."
"Man would have you change
To suit his frame of mind;
Take away your freedom
With a chain that binds."

"I am the only one
That always stays the same;
Who is by your side,
When you speak My name."

"I am ever with you
To wipe away each tear.
I love you as you are,
So put away your fear."

"Now lift up that chin
And let your smile impart
That you have found My love
Lives forever in your heart."

"Renewed"

"Come, come," beckons the Master,
"Be still and abide with Me.
I would lighten your load
Of care, so you could be free."

"Tarry just a while
And company with me.
Learn about God's truths,
As I tell them quietly."

"Then, as you go your way,
Anyone can see;
Your life has been renewed
By spending time with Me."

"My Child"

Master, hear me as I pray
For this child of mine;
Grant him understanding,
Love and peace of mind.

Ease all of his tensions,
Meet his every need;
With Your healing touch
Make him whole, indeed.

He needs to know for himself
That you love him, too;
And see the blessings he receives,
Truly come from you.

"Trust"

The Christ is with me always, He is my constant guide.
He loves me so very much, this fact He does not hide.
He leads me in paths of righteousness and by the silver stream,
Up the mountain trails, the climb does endless seem.

But He had planned this journey carefully all the way;
To follow His every guidance is my task throughout the day.
So I go on in faith believing, however the path might lead,
Because I know the Master will provide my every need.

He gives me joy and gladness to lighten all of my care.
With Him I know such safety, this friend who is so rare.
Forever now I will go on to do the will of the Master;
Helping all of His people learn there truly is a hereafter.

"God's Love"

God has such great love for us,
Not limited in any way.
He just keeps pouring it forth
Throughout day after day.

From early in the morning,
Through the darkest night,
He shows how much He loves us
With His eternal light.

He gave us eyes with which to see
The beauty of the flowers;
He gave us ears to hear
The wonder of the showers.

The amount He gives is endless,
We could never name them all;
They are combined with love divine,
The greatest gift of all.

"Master Teaching"

As they listened to the Master
When He taught in Galilee,
Many eyes were opened;
Many began to see.

They beheld the Christ
And then could understand,
The lessons that He taught
About immortal man.

He opened ears to hear
The voices of the past.
Teaching that life goes on;
It is the thing that lasts.

He taught the ways of the kingdom
And how to commune with God;
How to treat our fellow man,
As through this life we trod.

His lessons are not outdated,
They are supreme today.
Follow this Master's pattern
In all you do and say.

As you gain in wisdom,
And you come to know
The Christ who lives within,
You take on His heavenly glow.

Then as you venture forth
To help all mankind,
He will heal and teach through you,
The power of God's love divine.

"In My Every Prayer"

Since Jesus has touched me
With a love that is so rare,
He is always with me
Telling me how He cares.

I do not need to search
For a listening ear
To tell all my troubles,
As He is ever near.

He understands my needs
Before I even ask.
Then gives me divine strength
To help me with my task.

Jesus is the answer
To my every prayer,
Because when I am in need,
He is always there.

"The Temple"

Within us is a temple
That is God's holy place.
You'll find it deep inside,
It doesn't take much space.

You don't have to beg
Or pay a great amount
To enter God's holy temple,
It's the attitude that counts.

You must stay ever humble,
Leave all thoughts of self behind,
For within the holy temple walls
Truths of God is all you'll find.

When you are truly ready
To enter the temple gate,
You'll gladly leave all carnal thought,
Not a moment you'll hesitate.

Worldly thoughts and your desires
Cannot enter sacred walls.
The gateway is very narrow,
You must bow before God's call.

Always ready and so willing,
With patient love He waits,
His hand outstretched to guide you
Through the holy temple gates.

Still yourself and just relax,
Release every thought and care.
The key to the temple gate is found
In love, humility, faith and prayer.

God Made This World For Us

God made this world for us,
For folks like you and me,
That we might seek his kingdom
And be as we should be.

God made this world for us
That we might live and grow,
Learn all we could about Him
So others we might show.

God made this world for us,
So live it day by day.
Take each trial and win it
Then peace will come your way.

God made this world for us,
It's really full of beauty.
Take time to enjoy it,
That is a part of your duty.

God made this world for us,
So take it come what may.
Rise above all trouble and regret,
He'll help us all the way.

"In The Mist"

The mist now is rising
To disclose a bright new day.
As I lift my thoughts to God
I ask for guidance for the day.

Awaken my senses, Lord,
That I might know what to do.
Not just how and where,
But also when and who.

Make the need apparent
So I won't have to wait,
To do the Master's will
And never hesitate.

To heal the sick and needy
And aid the sad of heart,
Whatever their need might be,
Let me know my part.

"Walk With Me"

Take my hand and come with me,
We will climb the mountain high,
We will tarry by the sea
And we'll reach up to the sky.

We'll wander in the meadow
And by the silver stream;
Along the busy highways
We'll pause a while to dream.

There will be peace and glory
In the setting of the sun,
As we venture onward
To see His work is done.

We will reach the highest heights
That ever have been sought,
And then we'll go still higher
To the place that Jesus taught.

Ever seeking wisdom
Will be our way of life.
Onward, ever onward,
Will be our aim in life.

The kingdom we are seeking
And the kingdom we shall gain.
It may take awhile,
But victory we will attain.

Take my hand,
I'm the leader of the way.
I'll guide you in the night time
And help you through the day.

There isn't any limit
To the things that we will do;
If we just keep reaching upward
Until our work is through.

Hand in hand we'll wander
Over the mountainside.
You, the faithful pupil,
And me, your loving guide.

The doors to the kingdom are open,
Before you is the way;
In silent meditation
At the opening of the day.

With Just A Word Of Prayer

Sometimes, when we are weary
And laden down with care,
The burden feels much lighter
With just a word of prayer.

Troubles seem to stalk us,
They are a lot to bear;
You can make them brighter
With just a word of prayer.

When it is dark and rainy,
The sun's not anywhere,
You can make it brighter
With just a word of prayer.

If you feel sorry for yourself
And not a thing seems fair,
Still yourself, get back in tune,
With just a word of prayer.

Times when God seems far away,
You feel He isn't there,
You can draw Him back again
With just a word of prayer.

He really never leaves us,
We separate ourselves with care.
Retune your consciousness
With just a word of prayer.

A Mansion By The Sea

Take my hand and
Come with me.
I will take you to
A mansion by the sea.

This mansion cannot be seen
By the human eye
Because the mansion is something
That is built by you and I.

When we tarry inside this place
For a little while.
We bury all our troubles
And then begin to smile.

God meant for all to have the peace
That fills your waking mind.
All we have to do to attain,
Is leave ourselves behind.

So we'll go inside this mansion
And find a room for us,
One that is filled with love
And has never heard a cuss.

Come and let me take you
Through the halls of time.
Let me help you find
The love that is in your mind.

This love is in your soul,
It was put there by our God.
It is so beautiful to behold,
And on it no one can trod.

This love of God will fill your heart,
Will fill your mind and soul.
This love of God will fill every part of your being
And make you completely whole.

God loves you so very much,
For you are His special child,
He has given you a spirit
That is sweet and mild.

Ask The Father

He would give to you all things,
If you would only ask;
Not one thing for Him is small,
He's equal to each task.

Give your life to the Father
And He'll give it back to you;
Ask Him to manifest
In all you say and do.

He'll use you as a channel
To help all mankind;
Our Father God who is so loving,
Who is so very kind.

I would fill you with words that
Tell of His love divine.
I would fill you with the spirit
Of these words that are so fine.

If I could find a way to impart
The abundance of His love,
Oh, my child, I'd give it to you,
Then you'd soar like the beautiful dove.

Take my hand and come with me
To the mansion by the sea,
And I will help you all I can
To show that there is God in every man.

"The Massalian Garden"

In the Massalian garden,
As Jesus knelt to pray,
His heart was very heavy;
He knew this was the day.
The hour was fast approaching
When He must go away.

"Father, give me strength;
No time for feet of clay.
I need Your assurance
That there is no other way
To show there is eternal life,
And with my people stay."

"If I must drink this cup,
I'll do just as You say.
Father, give me strength
So that my will may not sway.
Grant me the power, God,
To proceed without delay."

"The Healing Fount"

I would like to take you
To a healing fount with me,
Make you straight and strong;
As perfect as can be.

You would be made whole
And add years onto your life;
Learn about the love of God,
Forget all of your strife.

In faith you need to open
The way to total healing.
One way to go about it,
Is to ask God while you are kneeling.

He will listen as you ask,
With His great compassion;
Then He will touch and heal you
With love that is everlasting.

"Step Inside"

Come inside with me awhile,
Have faith in all I say.
I will not leave you all alone,
My love is here to stay.

I've put a circle of protection
Around your very soul.
Know how much I love you
And want you to be whole.

Come apart a little while
And my peace you will find.
It will mend your broken body
And heal your troubled mind.

Christ is no longer on the cross,
From death He walked away.
He is always at your side,
Even when you stray.

I wish that you would turn within
And still your troubled mind.
The comfort, strength and love you seek,
In peace you'd surely find.

"The Door Is Open"

The doorway now is open,
Step inside my friend.
You asked for help and guidance,
Your pleas are at an end.

You sought the Master's hand
For showing you the way.
You sought the Father's will
In all you do and say.

You knocked upon heart's door
For answers from within.
Your knocking was persistent
And entrance, you did win.

When all fear you do cast out
Because of faith in Me;
And you trust without a doubt,
Then in Truth—You are set free.

"My Morning Garden"

In the garden in the morning
I pause awhile to pray.
I feel the Master's presence
And I long to stay.

To spend more time with Him,
Seems to be a growing need.
He lightens all my cares
And brings me peace, indeed.

I would tarry in the garden
Throughout the live-long day,
Just to be with the Master
If He would bid me "Stay".

But He tells me to go forth
And help those who want to see
A better way of life
And learn of eternity.

So I'll linger in the garden
Each morning for a while,
Because the day will prosper
If begun with the Master's smile.

"A Simple Truth"

May I instill in you this day
A very simple truth
If you will affirm life
You will find new youth
I told you it was simple
And if you practice every day
You will have a new outlook
When you earnestly pray

"*Forever Remember*"

God is the answer
To your every need.
Listen for His guidance
Before you do proceed.

Let His will be yours
In all that you do;
Then the love of God
Will come shining through.

He will guide your steps
Safely all the day
When you try to live
In His holy way.

You need never worry
How your life will grow
If seeds of happiness
Are all you ever sow

Always remember
You get what you give;
Your harvest is known
By the way that you live.

"My Fondest Dream"

To work and live with Jesus
Is my fondest dream.
I know that it will be fulfilled;
It's part of the Father's scheme.

The Father bids me "Come,
Walk this way with me.
I want you to tell my people
All about eternity."

"Be an open channel;
Do just as I ask.
I will give you strength
To finish every task."

"The path ahead opens
As you go along
With praise in your heart,
And on your lips, a song."

"Tell them of the kingdom
And of things above;
How I do forgive them,
That I am a God of love."

"Speak always with a smile,
Be gentle with everyone;
Then they will come to know
You walk with the Father's Son."

"Christ Is Always With You"

The Christ is always with you,
He does not walk away;
So trust Him when He tells you
"My love is here to stay."

Linger with Him in the morning,
Thank Him for your daily bread;
Know that He will heal you,
As by His way you're led.

He guides you as you journey,
He loves you as you sleep.
He comforts you in sorrow
And your loved ones He does keep.

Your painful times are over,
Your doubts are at an end.
Realize His goodness
And count Him as your friend.

"My Path"

As I walk along the narrow path
That leads through eternal life,
Everything grows brighter
When I overlook the strife.

I am so very glad
That God has let me see
There is no end to living;
That there is eternity.

Now there is no sad feeling
For things I've left undone,
Because now I know I'll finish
With another rising of the sun.

My task is laid before me,
And as I go along,
The way will be made lighter
With just a little song.

And as I sing His praises
My cares will go away;
Knowing I can begin again
Every single day.

"Guide My Feet"

Lord, please guide my footsteps
Throughout this lovely day.
Help me to be kind and loving
In all I do and say.

May I become a pattern,
As Jesus was long ago,
Of the way we should live;
That others I might show.

Mold my life, dear Lord,
Closer day by day.
Until nothing can be seen
But the glory of Your ways.

Make me ever humble,
Treading the narrow way.
Always ready to do Thy will,
Forever and a day.

"Til Days Work Is done"

The morning has come, the dawning is near;
Time to realize there is nothing to fear.
Quietly now, as the day has begun,
Rest in His peace 'til the day's work is done.

Don't try to rush; there is nothing to gain
By running about and going insane.
Stop now and then, take time to pray;
Then you'll find more time in your day.

Leave it to God, don't take it away;
He loves you and will help if you take time to pray.
God loves you and wants you to have peace of mind,
But you'll never have peace 'til you leave cares behind.

Set aside all your worries, put God in your life;
Love Him and trust Him, leave your troubles and strife.
Don't doubt for a minute, each hour of the day,
He loves you and will help you if you just open the way.

"Morning Worship"

Morning is a time for worship
And with it comes the dawn;
Awakening things that have been asleep
For so very long.

When you begin to feel
A reverence from deep inside
As you watch the world awakening,
God cannot be denied.

You will start to understand
For the very first time,
Everything that has been elusive;
That didn't seem to rhyme.

All things begin to drop in place;
Doors will open wide,
And the laws of nature
Their secrets no longer hide.

For now you have the keys
To unlock the doors of time.
God has given you insight
To teach His way divine.

So worship in the morning
And God will start your day;
Then remain beside you,
Blessing all you do and say.

"His Worth To Me"

I would love to tell you
How much Jesus means to me,
But there doesn't seem to be
Enough words in my vocabulary.

When you come to know Him
As a friend divine,
You will have this same problem
And then understand mine.

So I will simply tell you
In words one more than three;
How much does Jesus mean?
He's everything to me.

"Spiritual Millionaire"

I know I am becoming
A spiritual millionaire.
The Father opens the storehouse
To answer each need and care.
Now I have begun to prosper
In every phase of my life;
The radiant substance of the universe
Wipes out financial strife.
God pours forth His substance
In an ever abundant way,
As I return my thanks
By serving Him each day.

"Treasures"

Some may search for silver,
Others may search for gold,
But the treasures that I seek
Are the truths that Jesus told.

The ones that I have found
Have changed my very soul;
Strengthened my faith in God,
Then cleansed and made me whole.

I will keep on searching
Until each one I find.
This is the purpose of my life;
All else is left behind.

When I have found these truths,
I will share them with the world;
Then all men will come to see,
In God, their life unfurled.

So if you seek for treasures
And want a helping hand,
Come with me to the Master
And commune with the Son of Man.

"Child Of God"

You are a child of God,
Not limited in any way.
Go forth and heal the sick
And much will come your way.

It is by the grace of God
That you have your very being.
Do all things as He commands
And you will continue being.

When you use the gifts of God
You strengthen them threefold;
As you grow to use them more,
Your faith will make you whole.

These are the words of Jesus
And they are meant for you,
Because you belong to Jesus
And He has need of you.

As you grow in meditation
You will begin to see
That nothing can hold you back
From here through eternity.

So now let's get busy
And straighten out your life.
Things take on new meaning
As you set aside all strife.

In God you live and breathe
And have your very being.
Make use of all you have
To help others with their seeing.

God meant for all to have insight,
Not stumble in the dark.
He has given you a candle;
Now you give them the spark.

"This Morning As I Kneel"

This morning, as I kneel
And begin to pray,
I ask that God's richest
Blessings rest on you today.

May your burdens lighten
And your cares release;
Giving your existence
A touch of the Master's peace.

I pray for God to heal
Your body, mind and soul;
Touch you with His love and
Make you truly whole.

Inwardly, I see you straighten
And your shoulders square;
Shaking off the past
And the load of care.

As the pain begins to drop away
I see you start to smile.
For now you really know
You are the Father's child.

"Open Your Heart"

As I paused to pray beside a waterfall,
I opened up my heart to my God, my all.

Father-God, please touch me with Your holy power;
Make me your disciple, now, this very hour.

I want to heal and teach Your way to everyone.
Help me to show Your people each is the Father's son.

Use me, Father-God, as a guiding light
To help men come to You out of the darkest night.

My life now is Yours to do with as You will;
I have no other purpose than Your law to fill.

Let the Holy Spirit fill my life today,
Blessing every breath and all I do or say.

As I travel through this world along the narrow way,
Your divine guidance will always light my way.

"No Need To Hurry"

Day after day people scurry about
Not taking time to pray.
The hustle and bustle goes on and on
As they keep ever seeking the way.

Then one day someone says
"Stop, rest here by the well.
Be still and take time to pray."
Then suddenly it's clear as a bell.

The light that couldn't be seen
Is shining brighter that day.
All it took to make it clear
Was a pause by the side of the way.

Let us take some time right now
To kneel down and to pray;
There never was a better note
On which to start your day.

When you begin the day with God
And attune yourself to pray,
Everything runs smooth it seems.
This surely is the right way.

So if your day gets hectic,
Stop—whatever the time of day.
Take a few moments with God,
In a pause by the side of the way.

"When Spring Comes"

Time wears away
The ledge of stone.
It will also take away
Heartache that you've known.

Time, as we may know it,
Changes many things.
It changes the seasons
And brings about the spring.

In spring you think about renewal;
The changing of the guard.
The softening of the ground
That has been frozen hard.

Your time of spring will come;
You'll blossom out full force.
Just take it as it comes,
God has planned the course.

You will teach of the kingdom;
All things that men must know
To live a better way of life,
These things you're bound to show.

The healing that is inherent
Must be shown to man.
God loves everyone,
And this they must understand.

His gifts He seems to give to some;
This is only true in part.
To all they would be given
If they would open up their heart.

Give and you shall be given
All the gifts you can receive.
The only thing He asks
Is that you truly do believe.

"Know The Truth"

You shall know the truth
And the truth shall set you free,
If you follow as I beckon
And come along with me.

There is no need to tarry;
This you've done for far too long.
Leave carnal things behind,
Come on home where you belong.

Can't you hear me as I whisper
Very softly in your ear?
Come and follow me;
Draw ever closer, dear.

I need you and you need me,
Together we're quite a team,
To bring God's word and love
In a never ending stream.

"The Holy Breath"

Jesus said to his disciples
Do not grieve because I go away.
I will send a comforter
And by your side she'll stay.

The Holy Breath will come;
She will teach you more and more.
And bring to your remembrance
All that I have said before.

There are many things to say
This age cannot now receive,
Because it cannot comprehend
The thing that I believe.

The Holy Breath will tell you
Of each perplexity;
All the mysteries of the soul,
Of life and death and immortality.

The Holy Breath is truth;
Listen well to what she'll say.
God's truth never changes
And cannot pass away.